Mirrored Affections

D. L. Valentine

WESTBOW
PRESS®
A DIVISION OF THOMAS NELSON
& ZONDERVAN

WestBow Press books may be ordered through booksellers or by contacting:

WestBow Press
A Division of Thomas Nelson & Zondervan
1663 Liberty Drive
Bloomington, IN 47403
www.westbowpress.com
1 (866) 928-1240

ISBN: 978-1-5127-3785-1 (sc)
ISBN: 978-1-5127-3787-5 (hc)
ISBN: 978-1-5127-3786-8 (e)

Library of Congress Control Number: 2016905977

Print information available on the last page.

WestBow Press rev. date: 04/08/2016

Contents

River of Life

There is a river that lies in the mist. Some find it well,
though others fail. Some walk along its banks
though never take a full drink
even though healing and life
are beneath.
It is a river that all must cross,
no matter the plight we pursue. Some drink for its knowledge,
others to be consumed of its virtue,
but all will have come to take a sip.
To some it is but a far reach,
yet to others a day's journey,
though we are all in its mist.

Christ's Embrace

Bestow upon me lily pads of grace

full of Thy righteousness.

Waves of loving-kindness shall I embrace.

To live servant to all that is good,

I will have embarked upon life's most precious gift.

To hear the echoing call in the hollow of my soul

is the most honorable call,

to be made manifest of God's creativeness

with all thanksgiving, for mercy hath spared me.

More than justified are His praises that fill the heavens.

Therefore, clothe me with wisdom, and shed me of self-righteousness.

A debt that can never be paid

is a trade for a love. No one can separate us from,

for this is the love of Christ.

The Good Shepherd

Lord, keep my eyes
and my mind from adverting.
Thou art my whole affection in life
Keep me near to Thy way,
for in it are peace and joy
Even though sometimes we do stray,
I know Thou art the way,
so keep my conscience clear.
Every ill thought be taken away.
May I be as a child in awe,
wandering through Thy kingdom's halls
listening with every breath,
anxious to pursue Thy precepts.
Deal diligently with me, O Lord.
Let Thy grace be upon my face.
Name me repairer of the breach.
Yes, keep me from dusk to dawn,
and please keep me, keep me, Lord!

Hands of the Potter

For what saith the clay to the potter

Or the stem to produce fruit

If the branch be not on the tree?

For lest ye abide in Him,

How then can ye see?

The potter's clay formed He

Thusly to fit Himself.

Can anyone guess our predestination,

Or have we clung to our vain imagination?

Foreign is the spirit of the Lord

To those who know not His love.

Benefits of Grace

Though we are sometimes abased,
Yet with simplicity of obedience we abound,
Triumphant even over ourselves
By the mighty works of His grace,
Persecuted by our offenders,
For these are those who brace our footstools.
Though wickedness spreadeth wide,
It dwelleth not in peace.

Hate and strife raise their swords against us,
But His love overrides them both.
Mournful are we over the sins of the world
That all, may be reconciled unto Christ.
Beat upon by the waves of suffering,
Comforted by the surety of God's might,
Daily our patience strives the more
While truth and faith are woven in the soul.
By the purity of His Word,
We are cleansed and refreshed.

Our eyes are set toward heaven,
But the blind eyes of unrighteousness cannot see far off.
Humbled by humanity,
Though I am exalted by wisdom and knowledge,
We who rest in the Lord are blessed,
For He giveth everlasting joy and peace.

Of Earth

Flailing our tails around in a whirl,
going about as headless squirrels, grunting and
raging when we should be shouting and praising,
lying and cheating while the devils
the one scheming.

Playing and sleeping, but really we're just
out whoring, laughing, and pretending.
But the drugs are still killing,
sitting, and waiting,
not adding up what you're paying.

Talking and analyzing,
not about the truth but about social standings,
hating, and killing.
Is this why we're living?

Searching and probing,
in the vain dark
is where you're groping.

Flailing our tails around in a whirl,

living in a vain, repetitive world.

Redeeming Time

O Lord, help them understand

the wages of sin, which they will condemn.

Blessed be that wisdom that confirms their ignorance.

Thus, may they redeem the time.

Prudence lacks where morals be not.

Take heed: the hot coals weight not your deeds.

Replacements are we of time's passing greed.

The monetary affections feed not the soul, but

rather water your thirst

by the goodness of His Word.

Feast upon His righteousness that

your days may be long,

For what hope hath any man

if he be not of God.

I plead, brother, call upon God

in thy weeping hour,

and He will deliver:

your displeasures healeth He all.

Suffering State

Lend unto me thy suffering state

that I may bow my head unto grace.

Instill in me thy fear,
for wisdom doth begin here.
Grant it that I may persist
to him who endureth and not to the swift,

for the day of salvation doth draw near.

A Woman of Virtue

Within the conscious womb,
A breed of nobility
Of the soul lay yokes of love.
Her tongue covered with knowledge
Overlaid of wisdom,
Clothed in a timeless bouquet of beauty,
Her mind accented by deep understandings of Life.
Soft waves of compassion pour out
Laughter enough to fill the heart,
Patience to endure, beyond strength,
character of Glamour, and poetic pose
Pronouncing her innermost extraordinarity,

This woman of immeasurable value,

For she was handcrafted of God

That all who came to know her

May look and see Christ.

Befriended

He befriended thee with a touch,

Though he'll betray you with his lust.

Like a descending spiral case,

Your inner transgressions plunge.

Betray not thyself.

Befriend not his touch,

For moral depravity comes thus, I say.

Be not a part of such.

Befriend not his touch.

My Father Who Art in Heaven

His joy maketh glad
   all who are of His kingdom.
His peace stills the troubled waters.
   His truth made a way for the
Lord's righteousness
   that I may walk in His way.

His grace enables us
   to partake of heavenly riches.
His wisdom cries out,
   and understanding takes hold.
His compassion reaches depths
   beyond my innermost core.
Yet born of flesh to save us from sin.

His love gave birth
   to charity without bounds.
His spirit is unsurpassed
   by any other orchard of fruits.
His power prevailed over
   captivity, leaving it captive.
Come now, and let us rejoice.

Enemy of Self

I multiply my troubles
every time I speak.
Easily beset by my own forward mouth,
I should hush up, I say. But do I?
No way!
Gotta get my two cents in. That's the way it is today.
It neither waits its turn
so others can speak—it listens not—
nor does it ever stop.
I try to hold it still
by covering it up,
but as soon as I relax my hand,
it's forwarding itself.
My sorrows increase every time I speak.
By now you'd think
I'd have a grip on this thing. Give it something to hold,
but will it keep it?
Oh no!
It waits in the wind
to see what catch it may bring next.
Neither will it speak
all that is rightly so.
I say, "Beware of this enemy,
for it can snare your soul."

And What of Today?

Tomorrow is our today.

Yesterday has passed away.
Our coming is behind our going.
Lead on a path beyond price.
We dove into it as a drop in a pond,
hoping to be submerged.
We surfaced headlong.
Stirred up and contrite,
we are not as we belong,
making up judgment in place of inconsistency.
Can anyone see how lame we've become?
Leaning on the thoughts of others
can do us much harm.
Crafty words and a vain heart seem
to be all we've become.
Stealing from behind us, our virtue is robbed.
Between their teeth
are our open wounds.
Grinning about as though shame were not,
we cry, "O Lord, please forgive us our sins,"
but then we pay the Devil to put it back again.
Wearing masked faces to veil our true conceptions,
we and the world, I find, are much too astride,
measuring our efforts against time's warped impressions.
We must work while it is yet day,
for tomorrow is not promised.

We have only today.

Thanks

So it is with thanks I enter the day.
Careful to remember God's enormous grace,
I take into account all my blessings,
for my trials and tribulations are only temporary.
By God's Word I am continually changed anew.
I measure myself not against the standards of man
but rather against the height to which God is able to raise my soul.
Therefore, I can do no less than serve
Him with my whole,
for God's love is ever-compelling my heart
that my soul may reach the standard of His likeness,
in which I will have found the key to my existence,
and with that comes everlasting, love, joy, and peace.
And so it is with thanks I enter each day.

Renew Your Mind

But the wicked are like the troubled sea: when it cannot rest. Whose waters cast up mire and dirt. There is no peace, saith my God to the wicked.

—Isaiah 57:20

We ourselves are at an unrest, for our sins trouble us within. They also proceed before us as stumbling blocks. We trip and fall over ourselves because we refuse to pick up the clutter and mess in our own houses, too lazy to clean up our spiritual house. We lie in it and sleep. Yet we want the Lord to visit such a place. We want His high appraisals, and yet we're too lazy to sweep the dirt off the front steps. We go to and fro every day, stepping over our own mess as though it were not there. God said, "Clean up your spiritual house. Seek me daily, pray, and fast, study, and meditate day and night. Come out from among the ungodly. Cleanse and separate yourselves. Refrain from pointing the finger at others. Rather pray and help restore, lest the same temptation befall you. Be not as the wicked, but be ye transformed by the renewing of your mind."

Strive

Let us dare to solidify

in adoration for which we strive,

Careful not to omit the precepts set up to guide us,

leaving behind the footsteps

we have tread upon.

We wallow no more in our tearful regrets

or the secrets of the past.

Grace has pushed them aside.

Strive for the prize.

So let us purge our intellect

from fraudulent intent

to receive the prize of the divine reward.

We must seek Christ diligently,

surpassing our former selves.

Let us press toward the mark,

purging all contentions, malice, and strife,

May our souls be married to the Lord?

Without fornication or pride,

We cannot reach the place of perfection

unless we first seek to be submerged in Him.

My Testimony

Tainted dreams of past, I had been
Trying to borrow what I could
From others' dreams,
Thinking it might patch my shadowed scene.
Though the way was dark, I fought it, not
Thinking happiness would follow therein.
Instead
Loneliness, disappointments, despair,
And fear sometimes would creep in,
Though I searched.
I knew not,
What to look for
Within my soul plead, no hope yet
Had I found
Then a flicker of light
Passed me by night.
As I looked on, I found myself drawn
until at last the search I'd foregone.
        "It's dawn at last."
There's a sunlight breaking,
through the window of my heart

Along the Roadside He Noticed Me

There passing along a two-lane highway, with gently sloping hillsides lined with endless miles of trees and evergreens,

I couldn't help but notice a brilliant red bush showing forth among the greenery. Singular in how it made its way through strength and persistence to push its way forth, among all the harsh thickery of the forest. Even so, it made its way to stand out among the roadside. So shall I be among the sinfulness of the world. That God looking on will stop and notice me. How will you be seen from God's view? Like the sinners of the world. Or the light that shines forth out of obscurity.

The Bridges of Life

Once again here I stand, gazing at myself at long glance.

Troubled still are the waters beneath the bridge,

Clinging to the railing as I cross.

Though still rough,

I try to look up, to steady my walk,

But the troubling waters draw my mouth a frown

With nearsightedness, I gazed out at the distance.

There, just beyond my sight,

A bead of opportunity lends out,

I lifted up my right heel to take a step forward

(And I would have too),

If but for the nail still stuck in my shoe.

Becoming

Will I ever become
That which I'm longing for?

If only I could see through heaven's eyes
To imagine within as it really is,

Then would my inner spring churn and Overflow,

My courage and wisdom would soar with delight.

Then surely I would become
More than I ever dreamed of,

And life's meaning would take
On a new and profound understanding.

My dreams and aspirations—will I become

One with God's plan and purpose

That my life will posses
A meaningful fulfillment
In a never-ending joy.

And so it is—I strive to become.

Optimistic

Optimist forever, will I be,
Never the loading gloom preceding me.
My worldly gain, speak not the value of me.

The work of a man's hands
Inscripts his legacy.
Why yield to time unseen?
Rather think on positive things.

Optimist forever, will I be,
To possess that which seems unintangible
To dare to go beyond my own expectations,
To emerge out of my own dream,
Having it look back at me. Optimistic forever, will I be.

Redemption

Deep in a wedge of depression I had sank
When the compassion of God's mercy
Cried out my name.
I felt it when it stroked
The pain of my heart,
Asking me, "Why not take my yoke
Upon thyself,
For this is what mercy?"
Said to my heart
I gave thanks unto His kindness,
And asked forgiveness of my sins,
For there were a multitude of them.
Then the redemption of grace
Stepped from the throne
To take away my sorrow
And bless me with joy
And renewed my soul ... once more.

Ease Your Mind

I know it seems like the more you pray,
The more drugs he seems to take,
But remember it's always darkest
before the dawn.
And that God will always answer an honest
and sincere prayer.
Believe Him at His word, for
He will not fail.
Remember faith is not what you see,
nor what you feel,
But what you believe. That God will.

Peace of Mind

Peace of mind, can it be found?
Only if we shut our mouths
Oh, but that can't be so.
We're too busy pointing our self-righteousness
at others, you see.

Peace of mind, can it be possible?
Only if we stop living like backseat drivers,
But that would take the fun out of
What frustrates us the most.

Peace of mind, can it be felt?
Only if we leave the business
Of others to itself.
Oh, but that will never do.
We get a kick out of dogging
Someone else's name about.

Peace of mind, can anyone have it?
Only those who hush and lie in His trust,
But that won't do for most,
For we don't like to admit
That we're emotionally frail
And can't boss ourselves.

Abundant Love

Even after all the laughter has ceased,

Even beyond compassions ever unfold,

My love for you shall go beyond that,

Even to the stretch of the sea.

As the soft breeze rustles through the trees,

So are my thoughts of you.

Even as sure as the sun shall set

And the moon shall rise,

So are my prayers that God be with your every step,

Even as knowledge is to the vast universe,

Even so is my love for you,

And as God's ear is to the cry of the sinner,

So shall I be to your needs and desires.

Even as nature renews it's self over and over again,
Even as the covenant of God is perpetual,

My love for you shall grow in an abundant proportion Without cease.

Confession

I wrote a letter to confession.
Forgiveness wrote me back
With a loud voice.
I cried, "O wisdom!"
Understanding said, "Here am I,
Ushering out to bring prudence."
Knowledge and I now sup at night,
Gaping open my window
For light to shed
Love transpired, to which I overcame.

Love Thine Enemies

Now everyone else has jumped ship,
I stand on this plank, balancing myself, Remembering
that God forsook me not
But granted mercy in my day of distress,
For my calamities were great before me.

So stand I on this plank, balancing myself, Daring not
jump ship, as done the rest, Remembering how God's
grace rescued
My ailing fate
And created hope in my destitute state.

So you see, I cannot jump ship,
As done the rest.
No matter how wrong or right I've been,
His kindness and mercy have kept me still. Therefore, I
stand on this plank,
Balancing myself,

Careful that I not harbor any hate, Neither fall
pray to unforgiveness,
For if I fall pray, what hope would remain. Therefore,
you see, I cannot jump ship,
As done the rest.
I must stand on this plank and balance myself.

Faith

Faith is a seed word
that when placed
in the heart and watered

shall yield its fruit.

Cherish Your Mother

Cherish your mother
for all the days ahead when you'll yearn for her words of wisdom,
spoken by her voice.
Cherish your mother
for all the times in life
that cold door got slammed in your face,
and she wrapped you in her loving embrace, soothing it away.
vw your mother
for all the times no one else understood,
but somehow she knew
just what you were going through.
Cherish your mother
for all the hard scarifies she's made—
not just so you had what you needed,
but your heart's desires as well.
Cherish your mother
for all the times you were spiteful, disobedient,
and broke her heart,
yet her love for you never changed.
Cherish your mother
for all the wonderful things she taught you
about life and how to live right.
Cherish your mother
for all the prayers that kept you safe from harm's way,
for all the prayers that blessed you and brought you through.
Cherish your mother
for all the times you were down on your luck
and out of sorts.
Then Mama would call, and she knew just what to say to cheer you up.
Cherish your mother,
for she's a gift from heaven. She's like an angel in the flesh,

filled with the love of God. A pillar of strength and one to console. Her love is of a fine-woven fiber that holds families together. Cherish your mother
deep in your heart, and show that you love her often and much.

For a mother is God's physical manifestation of His love for us.

Deeply Yearning

To all who have a desire,

To all with a dream yet unfulfilled,

A salutation and words of hope

To the blesseth that mourn,

To all that strive beyond their means,

Disquieted of themselves,

Even the misfortunate of circumstance

Strive for the fullness of what faith is.

Believe in the purpose of your whole existence,

Stopping at nothing in pursuit of truth,

Knowing it is the life force of reality,

An ocean of deep compassion.

Wells for you,

A realm outside of circumstance exists

To whom believes,

To all who yearn deeply.

Oh, Wife

Oh wife, where art thou, oh wife!
Oh wife, I call unto thee,
    But thou answerst not.
Was it not I, that brought you precious jewels?
Did I not soothe you in times of trouble?
    But still you answer me not.
Yea, have I loved thee with an everlasting love,
    Will thou not beseech me, oh wife?
When the tempter came to swallow thee up,
    Was it not I that upheld your heart?
Times when your feet would slip, for fear thou had fallen away.
    With my wings I gathered thee up into the father.
Thou was brokenhearted, but I restored thee and
    gave thee a new heart.

Oh wife, where art thou, oh wife!
Thou wakest in the morning, and
    you speaketh not.
You walk past me as though I wasn't there.
    Even though it was I that put the joy in thine heart,
I poured my spirit into thine soul.
    With a pure love have I loved thee.
How long, oh wife, how long
Will ye not return my love
From afar brought I fine linens and remnants and clothe thee.
Neither did I leave you without shelter,
    But built thee a house in which to dwell.

Oh wife, where art thou, oh wife!
　　Answerst thou me!
Why is thine house so unclean?
　　And thine remnants spotted with dirt?
With my blood I cleansed thee,
　　Washing away every blemish
　　That all who look upon thee
　　Might see truth and grace everlasting.
This and more have I done for thee,
　　Will thou not entreat me,

For I am lonely in heart.
If thine would only humble thyself unto me,
　　Wisdom and knowledge would be at thine feet.
　　I made a lasting covenant with thee, and thee with me.
　　Where are thine prayers and thanksgiving?
Where is the fasting and meditation thou promised me?

Oh wife, oh wife, where art thou, oh wife!
I supplied thee good fruit to eat.
Thine cup I filled again and again.
　　Neither have thy cupboards ran dry.
Why will ye not feed me?
　　For ye have been given bread and water that
　　thou shall never thirst nor hunger.

I've given thee an excellent seed in which to multiply,
　　An inheritance more abundant than all the kings of the earth.
　　And still ye won't beseech me.
What then shall I do with thee?

Oh wife, long will thou continue this whoredom act.
Grieve me no longer. I can take no more.
Thou cans't not hide,
　　For I am in thee.
My breath is the life that breaths in thee.

Oh wife, oh wife, why doest thou not answer me?
Has sin caught thy tongue
That thou cannot speak?
Oh wife, oh wife, where has thou laid thine heart?
Doeth it lay in the temple of holiness.
    In the house which I built?
Or have ye laid it among the worldly?
    Know ye not, that your heart belongeth unto me?
Thy ransom have I paid, yea thou belongest to none other,
    None other shalt thou, love or serve.
    For there is none other to redeem thine
heart. My love is everlasting,
    And to whomever, oh wife, that will return this love
    Shall reap eternity.
Answer me, oh wife, that I may set the flame of fire to
    thy breast.
That the light from my glory will shine round about.
And I will make thee to mount up with wings,
    Like unto an eagle, to soar with me on high.
Free at last shalt thou be, if thou will only answer me.

Oh wife, oh wife ...

The Prize

I search for what men seek
Though few find.
I go where the thoughts of man
Cannot hide
To journey on a road of vastness,
To drink from the pool of eternity,
Where the latitude of faith
Breaths the breath of hope
And the offspring of joy continually
Renew itself,
Where the heaviness of heart
float as sticks upon water.
Yes, I journey to a place
Where the boundaries of intellect
Go beyond the probe of the imagination.
I need neither wings nor propellers
To set my soul aflight,
And time will age me no more.
A perpetual flow of blessings
Shower upon my head
My bones shall never be chilled
By the wind,
And the sun will never scorch my skin
Yes, I journey to a place
I needn't be rich or poor, for
All is set free and are at liberty.

Will you come with me?
On a journey in time and in place,
Where seas have no shores,
And clouds suppress us no more,
Established as an elect *ah*,
The wonderful providence of God.
(Yes, I journey to a place.)

Change

Struck by enthusiasm, though reluctant
 because of fear

Strangely enough,
 I live in this place

I fight and wrestle with myself all the
 day

Over what I will and will not say.
 What to think

I ponder these things
 With my hope in a clinch,

Like a kind loving, bright, but
 homely girl

To look at is not much appeal,
 But her attributes are far beyond price.

Others may see me as
 Looking through a dense fog,

Mirrored in are all my affections,
 Kept well by murmuring fear.

I long the day,
Hoping for a siege of liberty.

Fruits

Obedience to God

Is the wave of peace,

And the road to prosperity

Is to seek His kingdom.

Trees of Righteousness

Prevail forth victories. Applause that the word of the Lord has spread abroad.

We stand forth as trees to bear His light,
To awaken others unto His salvation
That the good word of the Lord is here.

And the trees of righteousness are nourished by it,
Its roots run deep,
Like the deep understandings in the mysteries of Christ.

Are we not anointed and appointed to build and restore?
Who will preach, who will teach God's anointed Word?
Who will proclaim his established truth to those who are lost,
And who will guide them in His precepts?

If not the trees of righteousness; then who?

Who shall hold up the shield of faith,
Where substance of hope become freely tangible?
Who will lay hands on the sick, so they can recover?
And who will give a word of season
From the vine of wisdom?

If not the trees of righteousness, then who?

Who will hold up a standard for the people
That the storms of life not wash them out to sea?
And who will tend to the vineyard,
And who plant new seed
That God may give water to those who are thirsty?

If not the trees of righteousness, then who?

Who will prophesy, who will teach that others will not
Leave here uncertain, but to know they have a purpose?
Who will shout it among the hillside?
Who will lift up there voice and speak forth?
And who will sound the warning?

If not the trees of righteousness, then who?

Who will lift there sight out of the lies of darkness?
Who will lead the way in the steps of salvation?
Who will stop to gather the lost sheep?
Who will search to bring back the one that drifted into the deep?
Or who will look on the poor, the hungry, or the widow so that they
are cared for?

If not the trees of righteousness, then who?

Who will fight for the unjust? Who will comfort the weary soul?
Who will bear the infirmities of the weak?
And who will stand in the gap?

If not the trees of righteousness, then who?

Was it not you and I, the anointed and appointed,
Whom God blessed and gave substance
And gave us His spirit of praise
That there be no more burden,

That we may be called the trees of righteousness
To be planted among the people,
That all who came to lodge among us
Will find strength within our circumference
Wisdom in our branches?

They'll see the good fruit that we bear.
They will find comfort under our branches
From the strife of life
And dew near the roots of our tree to nourish and refresh.

If not the trees of righteousness, then who?

Was it not us whom the Lord brought forth
To bring the Word unto the meek,
For who is there to lift up their voice
That the offspring of joy may continue to renew itself
So liberty's bell may ring the sound of truth?

If not the trees of righteousness, then who?

Who then shall preach the transcending Word of Christ
That our minds are no more chained to condemnation
But are now equipped to receive the revelation of God's grace?

If not the trees of righteousness, then who?

If Only I Had Listened

There I was in the mist of the storm.
Seemed all things in life were blown past
And beyond my grasp.
I feud with the wind just to hang on.
Quickly approaching me were my enemies, traps,
And snares.
I was bombarded by the mass confusion
And disillusions
With my head bowed down
As I explained it all to God Quietly, God looked upon me
As He listened on.
Day after day, I looked for you to rescue me
To calm the storm, to arrest my fear.
Now that I sit all worn and torn,
What will ye say now!

With compassion God spoke,
"I was there, warning you before the storm.
Come in from there worldliness, called I unto you,
Before the wolves devour you whole.
I sent My light to guide you out,
But you neither looked My way nor answered me.
More than deliver you,
If you had listened,
I could have spared you.

Mind Snare

Warped and distorted, my emotions hang loose.

My mouth is clinched tight,

For I am unable to speak.

The winding, twisting turns of my thoughts

Have woven my mouth shut.

Deep within, the yearning and churning persist.

How shall I ascend from this depressed state?

I think to myself all the day

How to undo this snare I'm in.

But to no surprise, though I've tried,

My yearning and churning persist.

Finally, I prayed to God

That He would take away this infirmity.

Instead He gave me strength to overcome.

To this day I thank Him,

For the abundance of His joy is with me still.

Dear Iola (Dear Sister)

We've come to say our good-byes
To a great tree of righteousness.
We are truly blessed to have lodged among her branches.
She nourished us from the nectar of her hearty council,
For we know her attributes were far beyond price.
She was a fortress of wisdom and understanding,
A marksmanship of discernment,
A cascade of generosity not only of her substance but of herself.
She was ever-vigilant to keep us under her watchful eye.
No one escaped her admirable attention.
God sent our sister unto us a watchful caregiver.
She made our needs her priorities.
Her strength and confidence were a steady breeze.
She was a mother, teacher, friend, confidant, sister, family physician,
and councilor.
No one left her presents, hungry or thirsty.
She set sail to council, to send you in a right direction,
A friend to the very deeps.
Yes, she was nearly everything to nearly everyone,
But above all else, she was a triumphant life.

Rekindle

How do I rekindle
The love in my heart?
How do I make way for God's own touch?
How is it that our lives
Have grown apart?

I remember we would
Pray and often talk.
We would sit for hours,
And I'd mediate your thoughts.

I was glad to hear from you,
And you longed for my voice.

How is it that our lives have grown apart?
What must I do to rekindle my heart?

Time

Deep within, you hid your fear
Sort it out, ya! Did I,
And freed you from its bondage,
Tired and perplexed you were,
But I strengthened and renewed your hope.
Disguised I your vulnerabilities,
Letting not the enemy pierce them.
Death tapped at your heels,
But swifter than death
Was my safety net.
In the palm of my hand,
Your life now held,
And by the power of my loving grace,
Thy span of breath strives on.

Her Stride

I was always proud and in awe of
The way she walked out into life.
Even though her heart felt unsure,
Her stride was forward with sincerity.
It was almost poetic how she glided
Past their pursed lips and eyes
Full of spying hate.
Disappointments she took in stride
Like puffing on a cigarette while waiting on a bus.
While his infidelity, she kept it hush.
I'm still stunned by how she pulled it all off.
Every day she had a smile for us,
Never letting on how much it hurt,
And when they looked at her as though
She wasn't enough,
She held her head up higher and broadened her step.
They did everything to raise her self-doubt
And cause her to fear—
The cold and chilling way
They would avoid her in conversation.
Meaningless stares gave away their intent.
Seared connections no true friends to care.
She graced that stride like a new pair of jeans,
In red-heeled pumps.
I could hear the base in her step
When she stopped to make a turn,
Keeping us abreast of the wisdom found there.
She could walk through a puddle of mess
With the grace of Freda Staire.
The dimensions of her love were like the facets
Of a jewel.

No matter what she had to walk through,
She held on to us two.
Her stride was through difficult terrain.
Very few times did she slip or lose her footing.

The one thing in her stride I wish she didn't have
Was the stepping aside.
A woman with this much heart and courage
Doesn't belong on a back burner.
Then one day it happened.
She walked into that place of knowing,
And not once did I ever see her look back.
Not a smear of regret was on the heel of her shoe.

She had taken life and put it on her terms,
And then I figured it out.
That's what the power of grace can do for one's life.

She came into the bare of her own.
A shade tree hung there,
And the breeze from it became words
That sang a new song!

In the end I asked her how she did it.

This was her reply:

> I sidestepped their jealousy,
> Moving right on pass their pride.
> I just closed my eyes as I passed,
> Jumping over the puddles of confusion.
> I ignored their arrogance
> With the truth of God.
> I just slid it aside
> As I wallpapered their lies.

The Man with the Gaited Walk

Be not as the man with a gaited stride.

Do not walk shackled along your journey.

But determine in your heart

Not to let the enemies' vices

Derail righteous endeavors,

Hidden within the scope of intent,

Not to burden the work of the cross

As if to no avail,

But to walk circumspectly that with all,

To do all, within all, toward all,

But with the rod of diligence,

Curve every fleshly appetite.

Spirit Evolution

How thy spirit poured upon my lips!
As divine as the sour grapes of wine
That sooth my inner soul
Do saturate the sore vex of my soul,
So is thy word that covers me
In my calamities of life.
Thy mysteries unfold as doeth
Sawn stitching upon tapestry.
Even more wondrous to me
Than under sounds of thy thunder
Is the arm stretch of your marvelous grace
And how mercy hath no bowels
Like an oceans which hath no floors.
Through perilous trials
Are we brought through Out all the ages.
Our finite human frailty,
It is with our utmost
We gather our minds and hearts
To understand a love
So magnificent and full of grandeur
That by the death of His Son, Jesus,
Freedom lay no more shackled,
And man was given power over sin
To become more than subservient clay
But to take that leap of faith (out of flesh)
Into spiritual evolution,
Into a world of eternity.

Storms

We all go through troubled times,

But surely not to our demise.
By hidden vines of enormous grace,
He strengthens us to weather the storms,
To grow a more measured faith
That in the distance we may see our way home.

Fight

Every day I arise. It's a fight,
A fight.
Every minute of every day,
I fight.
Every second of every minute,
I fight. I fight.
Every minute of every day of every second,
We are engaged in a battle,
A battle against good and evil.
We battle against our own actions
Through intents and emotions
That our situations in life do not Overcome us,
That we don't allow ourselves
To succumb to death's evil plans,
To keep ourselves balanced over the
scales of righteousness,
That we lean not toward evil deceptions
But stay in the mind of Christ.
Every day I arise. I fight. I fight.

My Heart

My mind lies in a place of unrest,

A truth resting deep within my soul,

Carving its way through my heart,

Etching its way though.

When will I turn to become

More aware of my inner self

That my life's goal is to strive

Past a weekly paycheck.

Whispering behind the gate,

My soul lies in wait.

Eternity's gate,

I can hardly anticipate.

Grace a Tow

To lie in the dark and contemplate with wishful tears,
Wounded souls left astray from the battlefield,
We need not settle into complexity.
Why waver over His fullness?
Is grace not enough to know?
All is accomplished to end.
Pour me out into Thy wiliness
That all my circumference
May be saturated with Thy substance.
Make it worthwhile,
Taking all and giving nothing back.
The sanctity of my soul,
Lily pods a tow.
Far off the light shines willingly,
Towing my soul into shore.
I have journeyed across a long wait
That I may share in this grace.
A profound understanding
Resonates in my human inabilities,
The liberating gesture of love,
As God pulled me from the stagnated corner
To live anchored to a substantiated grace.

Going Though

You have a choice.
You can go through kicking and screaming.
You can go through
Murmuring and complaining.
You can wallow in self-pity
Or depress yourself by thinking You have a choice.
Remember, it's not what you go through but how.

Iniquity

I compass myself about with

The weariness of my own iniquity.

Try as I may to shield my inner flaws,

But the anger of my frustrations keep erupting,

Exposing my inner wows.

Praying with all my might

To believe God at His Word,

Yet again my mustard seed's growth

Is clouded over by iniquity.

Iniquity is like trying to keep money

In a pocket that has a hole.

It's the little sins that rob us

Of our fullness in Christ.

Name Calling

Put on your shield that you may
Ward off their fiery darts
When they go off unjustly.

Pray for more grace that you not
hold it against them

When they mistreat you.

Put in play your long-suffering,

But when you have doubts,

Faith will secure the mystery,
And feelings of hate, we give no place.
It's by love that He has drawn us.
Remember, God's grace wasn't
Just for one but to all who have fallen
from their shelves.

Warped

Warped and distorted, my emotions hang loose.

My mouth is clinched tight,
For I am unable to speak.
The winding, twisting turns of my thoughts
Have woven my mouth shut.
Deep within, the yearning and churning persist.
How shall I ascend from this depressed state?
I think to myself all the day
How to undo this snare I'm in.
But to no surprise, though I've tried,
My yearning and churning persist.
Finally, I prayed to God
That He would take away this infirmity. Instead
He gave me strength to overcome.
By the arm stretch of His grace,
He has secured my heart in place.
Let it be settled in heaven
With absolution—
The ongoing profuse love Christ has for me.

Roads of Destiny

Don't be discouraged because things didn't work out.

Sometimes the things we want just aren't for us.

Be happy in knowing God will lead us on a right path

Beyond that which discouraged us

To that which can

Propel us toward the reward of our destiny.

Keep in mind there's a better road you'll

be on not long from now.

Gardening of the Soul

I shall climb the hillside

And stretch my wingspread to love my fellow man,

Reaching down, pulling up the darkened root

That feeds his insight,

To be planted in a green garden having shoots of offspring, yielding fruit.

Yes, He shall pull him out from the field of thorns and weeds.

No more wondering into the bucket of dross,

Being burden down with hate and sinful intentions,

But to love the light of the Lord

That draws every man.

Slender of Hope

Motivation comes from within.
It's that place in one's self that strives to exist.
It's the splendor of hope.

I have a splendor of hope in me,
And it has chosen my destiny.

Pounding daily to reach the forefront,
To share its splendor,
My heart clinches tight,
This thorny ache

That it may break free
To speak for itself,

For it knows more than I
What it wants to say.
If only it were free to convey
This splendor of hope,

For its great mystery
Holds purpose for us all.

Hope

At first it was small, just a shy thought
There in the corner of my mind,
But then it began to grow.
Not yet tangible though but still a thought,
I began to reach for ways to yield its possibilities.
I pondered its growth. Look!
It had grown into hope.
Like wind, it blew open
The shutters of my inspiration
And gave rise to the borders of my ambition.
I saw it when it stepped out of the shadow of hope
Into the brightness of expectation
That the dream may ripen.
The vine of hope had produced the fruit of tangibility.

Printed in the United States
by Baker & Taylor Publisher Services